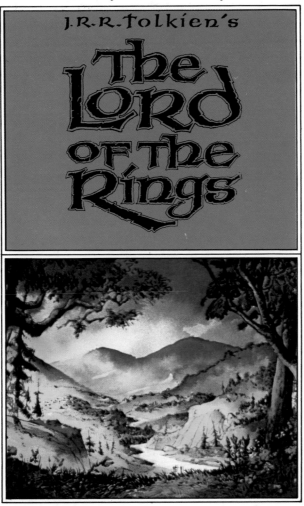

the film book of

J.R.R. Tolkien's

The Lord of the Rings

Over 130 pictures from the Fantasy Films presentation
of The Lord of the Rings Part One, with a text based on the film script.
Produced by Saul Zaentz. Directed by Ralph Bakshi.

METHUEN TORONTO

Gandalf the Grey,  wisest among wizards of Middle-earth, knew well the history of the One Ring:

'Long ago, the great Rings of Power were forged by elven-smiths. Nine of them were given to mortal men, seven to dwarf-lords, and three to the tall elf-kings. Word of these Rings came to the Dark Lord, the terrible Sauron. And, deep in the fiery depths of Mount Orodruin in the land of Mordor, he made One Ring which would rule the others.

'Through the power of this One Ring, the Dark Lord could become master of Middle-earth. But before he could complete his conquests, Men and Elves attacked his stronghold in Mordor. A young prince of Men, Isildur by name, faced the Dark Lord in single combat. He slashed at the hand whose finger wore the One Ring, so that the finger was hewn off and the Ring fell into the hands of Isildur himself.

'With the loss of the Ring, the power of Sauron the Dark Lord fell away almost to nothing. Yet it was ordained that while the One Ring remained in existence, Sauron's spirit would live on.

'Isildur soon fell upon evil fortune. He and his men were ambushed near the great river Anduin by a band of Orcs, foul creatures of Sauron. To save himself he

2

slipped the Ring on his finger, so that he became invisible, such being a power that the Ring conferred on its wearer.

'Still invisible, Isildur plunged into the waters of the Anduin. But the Orcs saw the splash and shot their arrows through the water's surface, so that Isildur was struck and killed, and the Ring slipped from his finger and dropped to the bed of the great river. There it lay for century upon century.

'Meanwhile the Dark Lord slowly rebuilt his power. He captured the Nine Rings of men, and of their owners he made Ringwraiths, dreadful shadow-shapes like black riders. These he sent out from Mordor to roam Middle-earth, searching for the One Ring. For if he regained it his power would become supreme.

'One day a small person named Déagol was fishing in the great river, when his line was caught by a fish so huge that it pulled him down through the water; and there he found a golden ring. Bringing it to the surface, he admired it; but when his cousin Sméagol saw it he begged to be given it, 'Because it's my birthday, and I want it.' And when Déagol would not give it up, Sméagol killed him and took it.

'Sméagol soon became utterly corrupt. He crept away from his people into dark caves at the roots of the Misty Mountains, where he sat gloating over the Ring. His shape grew foul and his old name was forgotten. Those who were aware of him knew him only by the gulping noise he made in his throat: '*Gollum*'.

'Long years later he was found by a hobbit. Hobbits are small creatures with fur upon their feet, and though they rarely travel far from their Shire, this hobbit, whose name was Bilbo Baggins, was on a quest for treasures with a party of dwarves (a party of which I, Gandalf, was the guide). Beneath the Misty Mountains, Bilbo Baggins found Gollum, and the Ring found Bilbo. It slipped from Gollum's finger and Bilbo took it, not altogether fairly, after a game of riddles with Gollum. By using the Ring to make himself invisible, Bilbo escaped from Gollum. Returning home to the Shire, he kept the Ring, though he wished it to be a secret.'

ilbo Baggins of Bag End, Hobbiton, was celebrating his birthday with a huge party. All the local families of hobbits were present: the Tooks, the Brandybucks, the Grubbs, Chubbs, Bracegirdles, Goodbodies, Bolgers and Proudfoots– or, as they preferred to be known, Proud*feet*. There was an immense quantity of food and drink, and the most marvellous fireworks, which had been supplied by Bilbo's old friend the wizard Gandalf.

Bilbo was a hundred and eleven, a great age even by hobbit standards, and he was not considered to be entirely respectable. Though it was many years since he had returned– and returned rich–from his strange adventures with a party of dwarves, his neighbours were suspicious of his odd ways. Nevertheless they gladly accepted his invitation to the party, and were even prepared to listen to his speech.

Bilbo stood on a chair. 'My dear People,' he began, 'today is my one hundred and eleventh birthday. I am eleventy -one today!'

'Hurray! Hurray! Many Happy Returns!' the hobbits all roared.

'I don't know half of you half as well as I should like,' continued Bilbo, 'and I like less than half of you half as well as you deserve.'

This puzzled them, and they tried to work it out to see if it was a compliment.

Bilbo went on: 'Though a hundred and eleven years is far too short a time to live among such admirable hobbits, I regret to announce that this is the End. I am going, *now*. Goodbye!'

At this, there was a blinding flash of light and a puff of smoke. The guests stared in amazement: for Bilbo had vanished.

While making his speech, Bilbo had been fingering the ring that lay in his pocket. At the end he had put it on, making himself invisible. The flash and the smoke were added for extra effect by Gandalf.

Still invisible, Bilbo slipped away from the uproar at the party and made his way into Bag End, his hobbit-hole. He finished his packing, took off his ring, and became visible again. He dropped the ring into an envelope which he sealed. At that moment Gandalf came in.

'Well,' said Gandalf, 'you have had your joke, and you have given the whole Shire something to talk about. Are you really going away?'

'Yes, Gandalf,' answered Bilbo. 'I feel like taking a permanent holiday. I hope you'll keep an eye on Frodo for me.' Frodo Baggins was his young cousin, who lived with him at Bag End. 'I'm leaving everything to him, except a few oddments.'

'Everything?' asked Gandalf searchingly. 'The ring as well?'

'Well, er, yes, I suppose so,' stammered Bilbo.

'Where is it?'

'In an envelope, if you must know,' said Bilbo impatiently, his face beginning to change.

'But it's mine, and I don't see why I should part with it. It's my own, my precious.'

'No!' cried Gandalf; and under his gaze Bilbo hesitated, then dropped the envelope containing the ring. Gandalf picked it up and put it on the mantelpiece.

A spasm of anger passed swiftly over the hobbit's face, but in a moment it gave way to a look of relief and a laugh. 'Well, that's it,' he said cheerfully. 'I'm off.' He stepped out of Bag End, waving goodbye to Gandalf. He was never seen in the Shire again.

he years passed, and Frodo Baggins lived a quiet existence as master of Bag End. One day he was dozing in his chair when there came a tap at the front door. Opening it, Frodo was amazed. 'Gandalf!' he cried. 'It's really you! It's been so long.'

'Seventeen years since Bilbo left,' replied Gandalf. 'I have come back to the Shire because there is something that you must know urgently.'

They went into the sitting room. 'It's the ring, isn't it?' asked Frodo, who had kept Bilbo's ring all these years, and knew that it could make him invisible. 'You always used to look like that when you talked about it.'

'Yes, Frodo,' answered Gandalf. 'It is the ring. Give it to me.' Reluctantly, Frodo removed the ring from the chain on which he wore it.

Taking it, the wizard said: 'Can you see any markings on it.'

'No,' said Frodo. 'There are none.'

'Then wait,' answered Gandalf, and suddenly he flung the ring into the heart of the fire. Frodo cried out, but Gandalf restrained him, and when the wizard removed the ring from the flames it was undamaged. Indeed it was quite cool to the touch, but strange writing had appeared on it. 'Yes,' said Gandalf slowly, reading these fiery letters, 'it is as I thought.' And he read aloud the words on the ring, translating them into the common speech:

One Ring to rule them all, One Ring to find them,
One Ring to bring them all and in the darkness bind them.

'This is the Master-ring, the One Ring of Sauron the Terrible. He lost it years ago, to the great weakening of his power. He greatly desires it – but he must not get it.'

Later that day, as afternoon drew towards evening, Gandalf and Frodo continued their talk, walking in the lane that ran from the front door of Bag End. Nearby they could hear Sam Gamgee, Frodo's gardener, trimming the grass with his shears.

'Perhaps', said Frodo hopefully, 'the Dark Lord does not know that his Ring has been found?'

'He knows, Frodo,' Gandalf answered. 'Gollum left his cave to follow the Ring himself. His journeyings were many, and the Dark Lord caught him and tortured him in Mordor, so that *He* learnt what ring it was that Gollum found, and how he lost it again; and *He* has heard of hobbits, and of this green and peaceful Shire; and *He* even has a name to think about, a name that Gollum had learnt from Bilbo – the name of *Baggins*.'

Frodo shivered. 'So it is as bad as that? Oh, Gandalf, what am I to do with the Ring?'

'The decision lies with you,' Gandalf answered.

Frodo thought for a moment. Then suddenly he looked up with hope in his eyes. 'I know, Gandalf!' he said. 'I will give it to *you*. For you are wise and powerful and good.'

'No!' cried Gandalf. 'This must not be. For wise I may be, and good too; but the Ring cannot be used for any good purpose. It is utterly evil, and with it I would be corrupted, and would become as terrible as the Dark Lord himself. Do not tempt me!'

Frodo sighed. 'Then I suppose I must keep the Ring, and guard it. But really I . . . I ought to go away somewhere, alone. For *He* won't bother the Shire, nor trouble my people, if the Ring isn't here, will he?'

Gandalf looked solemnly at the hobbit. 'You have a generous nature, Frodo,' he said. 'And I am afraid that you are right. You will have to go.'

Suddenly Gandalf froze, as if listening intently. A moment later he sprang towards a bush, parted it, and revealed Sam Gamgee. 'You!' he roared. 'What have you heard?'

'Oh, help!' cried Sam in terror as Gandalf grasped hold of him. 'Mr Frodo, sir, I didn't mean no harm. Don't let him hurt me, don't let him turn me into anything unnatural!'

'Answer him, Sam,' said Frodo. 'Why were you listening, and what have you heard?'

'I couldn't help it, Mr Frodo,' Sam answered. 'I was clipping away at the grass, and all that talk came to my ears. I heard a deal I didn't rightly understand, about a Dark Lord, and Rings, and Men and Dwarves and Elves. Oh, Mr Frodo, I would dearly love to see Elves.'

A thoughtful smile crossed Gandalf's face. 'And so you shall, Sam Gamgee,' he said. 'So you shall.'

Sam fell speechless; his mouth opened and shut, but nothing would come out of it.

Gandalf turned to Frodo. 'It really does seem the best plan,' he said. 'You should go to the Elves first, to the Last Homely House at Rivendell, at the foot of the Misty Mountains.

You must tell everyone here that you are moving away-let's say, to set up house in Bucklebury across the Shire - with those cousins

of yours, Merry and Pippin. But however you manage it, do it soon, by your birthday at the latest. I should be back by then, but I must go south now, for I have business of my own to attend to. Be careful, Frodo.' The wizard turned to go. 'Oh, and you are to take Sam with you, as your helper and servant. Goodbye!'

'Goodbye, Gandalf,' Frodo called to the departing figure of the wizard. He sighed, thinking of the long and difficult journey that lay ahead of him, of the Ring, and of the Enemy who longed to possess it again. He knew of the Last Homely House at Rivendell, for Bilbo had dwelt there during his journey with the dwarves to recapture their treasure. It was a place of peace and safety, but it was far from the Shire, far to the east.

A moment later, Frodo's thoughts were interrupted by Sam Gamgee, who could keep silent no longer. 'Me, sir?' he cried. 'Me, go and see Elves? Hooray!'

rom the Shire, Gandalf took the south road that soon left the green lands of the hobbits and crossed wilder and more desolate country.

He too had a long journey to make; for, now that he knew that Frodo's ring was indeed the One Ring of Sauron the Dark Lord, he had to determine what must be done with it. Even if Frodo made his journey safely to the Elves at Rivendell, this could not be the end of the matter. For the Dark Lord would certainly find it there at last, and would take it by force. Something must be done which would prevent him from ever possessing it again. But what?

Gandalf had decided that in this great matter he must be advised and aided by the head of his Order, Saruman the White, who was especially learned in the lore of the Elven-rings and the devices of Sauron.

This Saruman, mightiest of wizards in Middle-earth, dwelt far to the south, at the utmost extreme of the Misty Mountains. Here, there lay a circle of sheer rocks which enclosed a valley as if with a wall, and this valley had the name of Isengard or 'iron-fortress'. For there were many artifices of iron within it, powerful machines and other devices of Saruman, who was skilled in such things.

And in the centre of Isengard stood the huge tower that was the fortress of Saruman, the mighty Orthanc.

This tower had not been made by Saruman, but by the men of Númenor, the western land that had been lost in the sea long ago. It was very tall, and had many secrets.

Gandalf came to Isengard. He rode to the foot of Orthanc, and came to the stair of Saruman. And Saruman met him and led him to his high chamber.

'So you have come, Gandalf?' said Saruman gravely. But in his eyes there seemed to be a white light, as if a cold laughter was in his heart.

'Yes, I have come for your aid, Saruman the White,' answered Gandalf. 'For, if I am not deceived, events are at hand which will require the union of all our strength. The Nine Ringwraiths have come forth from Mordor, and are searching for the One Ring. And the Ring has been found, though not by them. For the moment it is in safe keeping. But for how long, I do not know.'

'And do you know where the One Ring lies at this moment?' Saruman asked.

'I do,' Gandalf answered, and fell silent, for he saw that a change was working in Saruman's face.

'You do?' went on Saruman. 'How long, I wonder, have you concealed this matter of the greatest import from me, the head of your Order? But no matter. I have not brought you into my tower to be instructed by you, but to give you a choice. For a new Power is rising, the Power of the Dark Lord. We may join with that Power; its victory is at hand, and there will be a rich reward for those who aided it. Or, better still, we ourselves could take the Ruling Ring, so that the Power would pass to us. That is indeed what I wish!' As he said this a terrible lust shone in his eyes. 'Tell me where the One Ring is!' he cried.

'Saruman,' said Gandalf, 'I will not. You have unmasked yourself. You have offered me two choices, and I will take neither. Have you others to offer?'

'I have,' said Saruman coldly. 'If you will not aid me willingly, you will stay here as my prisoner, until you reveal to me where the One Ring is to be found.'

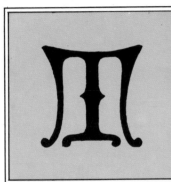

he weather was fine and the day bright as the hobbits set out on the first stage of their journey. 'Mr Frodo,' said Sam Gamgee, 'I don't feel right, going off without Gandalf. I wish we could have waited.'

'So do I, Sam,' answered Frodo. 'But I'm sure he'll catch up with us.' He turned and glanced back into the hollow behind them, where the morning mist was rising. 'I wonder if I shall ever look down into that valley again,' he said quietly.

All that morning they rode on merrily enough, chatting or even singing, and stopping now and then for a bite of food. But later the weather turned chilly and the sky grew grey, and this lowered their spirits a little.

They had met no other travellers on the road, so it was with some surprise that, towards sunset, they heard hooves approaching behind them.

Frodo turned – and was suddenly afraid.

'Quick,' he said, 'let's get off the road. I don't want to be seen leaving the Shire.'

'But it might be Gandalf,' said Pippin.

'Then we'll surprise him,' answered Frodo. 'Hurry!'

The hobbits ran down into the bushes, leading their pony. 'Under here,' whispered Frodo, pointing at the great roots of a tree.

They heard the horse come level with them and stop. The rider dismounted. His face was not visible, but he wore a great black cloak and hood. He seemed to be looking for something – or

rather, *sniffing*. Frodo suddenly felt a great desire to put on the Ring.

He began to move his hand to where it lay in his pocket. But just then the black rider straightened up, turned, went back to his horse, and rode off.

The four hobbits sighed with relief.

'Well, Frodo', said Merry, 'that settles it. We're coming with you, and not just as far as Bucklebury. You haven't fooled us with your talk of "moving house". We know about the Ring, and your journey; we guessed part of it, and forced Sam to tell us the rest (don't be cross with him!) and we're going too!'

So they went on their way, beyond the edge of the Shire, and came at night to the village of Bree, where they took a room at the Prancing Pony Inn. To the landlord, the plump Barliman Butterbur, Frodo gave his name as 'Mr Underhill'. After they had eaten and drunk their fill, Merry decided to go out for a sniff of air. He left the bar parlour, and it was just then that one of the company called for a song from the hobbits. Not wishing to be ill mannered, Frodo climbed on to a table and began the old song about the Cat and the Fiddle. But when he got to the line 'The cow jumped over the moon', he lost his head and took a leap in the air. He missed his footing and fell, and as he did so – he vanished! The Ring had somehow slipped on to his finger.

There was amazement, and some whispering amongst unpleasant-looking fellows who were sitting in the corner. Frodo managed to crawl away and take off the Ring without being seen. Then he, Sam and Pippin made themselves scarce as quickly as they could.

'Well,' said a voice behind them as they came out of the bar parlour, 'you are

being very careless, Mr Frodo Baggins. No – you needn't deny the name.' The speaker was a tall weather-beaten man who had been watching them all evening. 'I am a friend of Gandalf,' he went on. 'He sent me to watch for you. You can call me Strider.'

Just then Merry rushed in, pale faced. 'Black Riders!' he panted. 'I have seen them, in the street! They nearly caught me.'

Strider stiffened. 'We must make plans,' he said. 'The four of you are to get rest while you can.

The night deepened. In the inn, the hobbits slept.

In the cold hour before dawn there came the distant sound of horses. A few moments later, outside the gates of Bree, a voice, thin and menacing, snarled: 'Open, in the name of Mordor!'

The gates flew open, and the shapes of Black Riders passed into the village.

The Prancing Pony Inn stood shuttered and barred, with not a light showing. Barliman Butterbur the landlord snored in his bed.

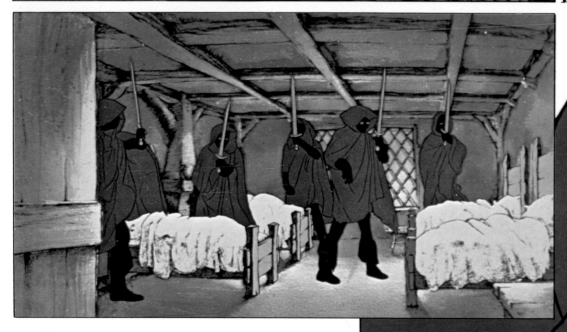

He did not hear the sound of stealthy steps, nor the creaking of wood as two of the black figures prised open the windows of the hobbits' bedroom. Then, in an instant, all the Riders were in the room, the cold steel of their drawn swords glinting with an evil and unnatural light.

In the four hobbits' beds lay four shapes. The black figures moved stealthily to the side of the beds and awaited the command. In a moment their leader, his red eyes glinting terribly in the darkness, gave the signal.

Down came the swords of Mordor, hacking and stabbing. Then it was over, and, with a low hiss, as of indrawn breath, the black figures left by the way that they had come. In a moment their hoofbeats could be heard passing into the distance. The window curtains flapped in the dawn wind, as the first grey light of day began to filter into the room.

Taking Strider's advice, the hobbits had slept on the floor elsewhere in the inn, having first stuffed their beds with bolsters and blankets to make them look occupied. When they saw what had happened they knew there was no time to lose.

'Though I am known as Strider,' their new companion told them, 'my true name is Aragorn son of Arathorn. With your consent, I will guide you to Rivendell.'

They set off, taking a difficult route across the Midgewater Marshes, which was both a short cut and (they hoped) a way of eluding their pursuers. They found they were not only in perpetual danger of sinking in the quagmires of the Marshes, but were constantly tormented by swarms of midges.

'How long will we be in these marshes?' Frodo asked, after they had been travelling for hours.

'At least two days,' Aragorn answered.

'Two days?' spluttered Pippin. 'I'm being eaten alive.'

For the time being they seemed to

have eluded the Riders. But once, at night while the hobbits were sleeping, Aragorn heard a low cold wailing far in the distance, and it was answered by another cry of the same kind. Frodo stirred and woke at the sound, and Aragorn saw the terror on his face.

They had set their course for Weathertop, a high hill where Aragorn had some hope of meeting Gandalf, or at least of finding a message from him.

'We should be there by nightfall, if we set a good pace, and if we do not stop to eat,' he said to the hobbits on the third day after they had set out from Bree.

Merry and Pippin groaned at this, and Frodo gloomily tightened his belt, trying not to think of food. 'If this goes on much longer,' he said, 'I'll become a wraith.'

'Do not speak of such things!' said Aragorn earnestly.

At that moment Frodo, who had turned to look back over the land through which they had passed, whispered, 'Aragorn, look!'

Far away, moving along the road, were five black figures.

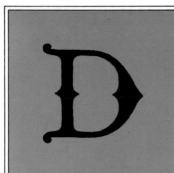

Despite what Frodo had seen, the hobbits and Aragorn reached Weathertop safely that night. Gandalf was not there. They lit a fire in a sheltered spot, and huddled round it. Everything was deathly still.

To cheer them, Aragorn began to tell the ancient tale of Beren, the mortal man who loved Lúthien Tinúviel, daughter of an Elven-king. But he had scarcely begun when Merry whispered: 'Aragorn, I thought I saw something.'

Aragorn peered into the darkness for a moment. Then he stiffened, and said: 'Stand close to the fire, and make a circle!'

They obeyed him, and took the blazing branches which he drew out from the flames. As they did so, tall shadows seemed to grow out of the darkness and approached them relentlessly.

Like his companions, Frodo was terrified, but his terror was swallowed up in a sudden desire to put on the Ring, and he slipped it on his finger.

As he did so, he vanished from his companions' sight. But he himself could now clearly see the Riders who had till then been mere shadows. The sight was terrible. Their eyes burned as they advanced on him.

Frodo drew his sword, but one of the Riders bore down on him, brandishing a knife which glowed with a pale light. Crying out, Frodo dived at this figure with his sword. But as the sword struck out, the Rider's knife came slashing down, and Frodo fell.

Aragorn leapt forward with a flaming brand in either hand, and the Black Riders turned and fled. But Frodo lay motionless on the ground.

Frodo's wound was in the shoulder. He did not seem to be seriously hurt, and soon opened his eyes, but Aragorn was anxious. 'It was an evil knife that struck him,' he said. 'A piece of it has broken off in the wound, and may be working inward. If it reaches his heart. . .Well, we must get to Rivendell as quickly as we can.'

They set off, Frodo riding on the pony while the others walked. He looked pale and ill, and swayed in the saddle. The pain in his shoulder seemed to him like the piercing of a poisoned icicle. To his eyes, everything around him seemed grey and misty. The faces of the others came and went before him, seeming distorted and barely distinguishable. He could only just hear the voices, as though from a long way off.

'Tomorrow,' Aragorn was saying, 'we will cross the Last Bridge. After that it is four or five days' journey to the ford at Rivendell.'

The next day passed, and they crossed the bridge without seeing anything more of the Black Riders, the terrible Ringwraiths.

But towards evening Frodo collapsed in the saddle. 'He can't go no further,' said Sam in desperation.

'He must,' answered Aragorn fiercely. 'Do you want *them* to take him?'

It was just then that they heard the sound of hoofbeats. Aragorn snatched the pony's reins, and they all hurried from the road to hide. But it was no Black Rider. Instead there came into view a tall Elf, his cloak streaming behind him. He was astride a great white horse whose harness was trimmed with bells. Joy shone in

Aragorn's face. He ran to the road, and called out: 'Ho! Legolas!'

The rider halted, and cried in greeting, in his own language: '*Ai na vedui, Aragorn! Mae govannen!*'

Sam stared with his mouth open. 'An Elf!' he said.

Legolas the elf had been sent from Rivendell to seek for them. Now he set Frodo on his horse, and began to journey back to Rivendell with them. 'There are five Black Riders close behind you,' he warned them, 'and we may find the others waiting in ambush.'

They journeyed on, Frodo swaying deliriously on the elf-horse. As he grew more sick, the very substance of his body seemed to change and become almost transparent.

At last the travellers came in sight of the ford where the road crossed the river into Rivendell. Beyond it, tall mountains climbed shoulder upon shoulder into the fading afternoon sky.

Suddenly there was the noise of galloping hooves behind them. Legolas threw a glance over his shoulder, then cried: 'Fly, fly! The enemy is upon us!'

The white elf-horse leapt forward, towards the water, bearing Frodo, while others ran down the slope to the ford as fast as they could. From the road behind them came five Black Riders. And now these were joined by four more, who had been waiting in ambush in the woods, just as Legolas had feared.

Frodo was almost through the ford when he saw, all too clearly, their terrible shapes.

'Come back!' their leader hissed at him.

'Come back! To Mordor we will take you!'

Frodo felt himself powerless. An almost irresistible force tempted him to put on the Ring and yield himself into their power. Yet he mustered his little remaining strength, and cried: 'By all the Shire, you have neither the Ring nor me!'

His horse carried him to safety, and at that moment there was a roaring of water. The river rose, and plunged down on the Black Riders in a raging cataract, sweeping them away. Then Frodo seemed to feel himself falling, and heard and saw no more.

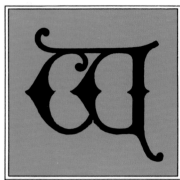

hen Frodo came to his senses, the first face he saw was that of Gandalf.

'Yes, I am here at Rivendell,' said the wizard. 'And you are lucky to be here yourself. You only arrived just in time: the knife-point had almost worked its way to your heart. But now Elrond, the master of Rivendell, has healed you.'

'The river rose up against – against *them*,' said Frodo, puzzled.

'Elrond commanded the flood,' said Gandalf. 'But the Black Riders have not been destroyed. They will return to Mordor and find new shapes to wear and new beasts to ride.'

'Where have you been, Gandalf?' Frodo asked.

'I wondered when you were coming to that,' said Gandalf. 'I was kept prisoner by Saruman, once the wisest of wizards but now a slave to the Dark Lord. He imprisoned me on the top of his tower, but he had not reckoned with the great eagle Gwaihir, who came in answer to my call, and bore me away.'

Frodo rested. Later, he was well enough to walk in the gardens and halls of Rivendell. Never before had he seen such beauty.

In one corner, a group of elves were gathered around a small figure who was reciting a poem. Frodo approached. 'Bilbo!' he said in amazement.

The old hobbit looked up. 'Hello, Frodo my lad,' he said cheerily. 'I was wondering when you'd appear.'

'Oh, Bilbo,' cried Frodo, 'have you been here all these years since you left the Shire?'

'There didn't seem much reason to be anywhere else,' Bilbo answered. 'It's a remarkable place altogether. But fancy that old ring of mine causing such a disturbance.'

Just then there was a sound of a bell, and Gandalf came up to them. 'The Council of Elrond is beginning,' he said gravely. 'Come with me, both of you.'

ll that morning, the Council of Elrond debated the matter of the One Ring.

Many were present. Elrond the master of Rivendell was there, and his daughter Arwen. So too were Legolas and many other elves. Others had come from far lands; among these was the dwarf Gimli, whose people Bilbo had helped to regain their treasure many years before. Gandalf was there too, and the hobbits. As to the race of Men, besides Aragorn there was at the Council a man named Boromir, from the land of Gondor beyond the Misty Mountains.

'In Gondor we are in grave peril,' Boromir told the Council. 'Already the forces of Mordor are attacking us.' He explained that he had come to Rivendell to seek for help because in a strange dream a voice had told him to do so, crying: 'Seek for the Sword that was broken.'

At this, Aragorn stood up. 'Here is that sword,' he said, putting the two pieces of his broken sword on the table. 'It is the weapon of Elendil, the father of Isildur, who was the king of Gondor long ago. I am their heir.'

Boromir stared in amazement.

'And now, Frodo, bring out the Ring,' commanded Gandalf. Frodo slowly held it up before the eyes of all.

'We must determine what is to be done with it,' said Elrond. 'We cannot keep it, for Sauron who forged it looks for it, and Saruman who envies it searches for it too.

It must be destroyed, and there is only one way in which that may be done.

No ordinary fire would melt it. It must be sent into Mordor, to the Fire where it was made – to Mount Doom.'

Boromir leapt to his feet. 'What foolishness is this?' he cried. 'Why do you speak of destroying the Ring? It could save all Middle-earth!'

'No Boromir,' said Elrond gravely. 'The Ring cannot work for good. It is Sauron's, and it is utterly evil. To wield it you would have to become like Sauron.'

'Our hope lies in that which you call foolishness, Boromir,' said Gandalf. 'For the Dark Lord will scarcely conceive of anyone wanting to *destroy* his Ring. He will expect us to use it, and that is what he will wait for. It is possible that because of this he may not notice the small, quiet feet carrying it – unused – into peril, into Mordor itself.'

38

'Small, quiet feet?' echoed Bilbo. 'Very well. It's plain enough what you mean, Gandalf. Bilbo the silly hobbit started this affair, and he had better finish it – or finish himself. Frightful nuisance, but never mind. When do I start?'

Gandalf smiled, but there was grave respect for the old hobbit in that smile. 'My dear Bilbo,' he said, 'If you had really started it, you might be expected to finish it. But you know that you only played a small part in the history of the Ring. Yours is a valiant offer, but one beyond your strength. This last journey of the Ring must be for others to make.'

Frodo sat silent, with a growing dread, as if he was awaiting the pronouncement of some doom that he had long foreseen, and which he vainly hoped might never be spoken after all.

An overwhelming longing to stay in Rivendell, by Bilbo's side and at peace, filled his heart. At last he spoke, and wondered to hear his own words.

'I will take the Ring,' he said.

Elrond nodded slowly. 'I think that this task is appointed for you, Frodo,' he said. 'The hour of the Shire-folk has come at last.'

Sam jumped to his feet. 'But sir, surely you won't send him off alone?'

Elrond smiled. 'You at least shall go with him, Master Samwise. After all, it is hardly possible to separate you, even when he is summoned to a secret council and you are not.'

Sam blushed. 'A nice pickle we've landed ourselves in, Mr Frodo!' he muttered.

After much discussion it was determined that the company escorting the Ring should be nine in number. 'Nine Walkers against the Nine Riders of Mordor,' declared Elrond. Legolas for the Elves, Gimli for the Dwarves, and Boromir for the Men would go as representatives of the Free Peoples, and this, together with the four hobbits, Gandalf and Aragorn, made up the Company of the Ring.

While preparations were being made for the journey, Bilbo came shyly to Frodo. 'I thought perhaps you might care to have these,' he muttered, handing Frodo his small sword and dwarf-shirt of specially precious ring-mail, which he had brought back from his own adventures. 'Take care,' he said. 'Good luck, and I shall expect to hear about every detail when you get back.'

It was now exactly mid-winter. They had planned to journey up into the

Misty Mountains and across a pass. But after they had travelled for some days the weather became terrible. It was only by a hair's breadth that they escaped a dreadful avalanche. 'The mountain itself seems to be attacking us,' muttered Frodo.

'We cannot go on,' shouted Gandalf against the wind and snow. 'We must travel through the mountains by another way. We will have to go *beneath* them — through the Mines of Moria.'

The dwarf Gimli looked up with smouldering eyes, his people had fashioned the great Mines of Moria, and he longed to go back there. But to the others, Moria was a name of evil omen. Even the hobbits, who knew little of it, felt a vague sense of dread. Only after much argument did they agree to journey by that way.

Towards dusk the same day, they came to a stagnant lake, by the side of which towered a cliff. In this there was a smooth face of rock, with no sign of crack or opening. Only the Elvish letters carved in it showed that this was the Gate of Moria.

Gandalf was puzzled. 'It is written in the Elvish letters: "Speak, friend, and enter." Some kind of password is needed to open the doors. But what is the word?' He thought for a moment, then cried '*Edro!*', which is the Elvish word for 'Open!'

Nothing happened. He tried word after word, in language after language. Boromir stared disconsolately at the stagnant water. Picking up a stone, he threw it into the lake. 'Why did you do that?' asked Frodo. 'I am somehow afraid of that pool.' Great rippling rings began to form on the surface.

Suddenly Gandalf roared with laughter. 'What an old fool I am! Now, watch.' And waving his staff he cried '*Mellon!*' which is the Elvish word for 'friend'. Sure enough, the rock face divided in the middle and a door swung open, revealing blackness beyond. 'All you had to do was say "friend" and enter. Let us go.' And Gandalf and the others began to stride forward.

But at that moment Frodo felt something seize him by the ankle. He fell with a cry.

A slimy tentacle had come out of the lake and grabbed him. Sam slashed at it frantically with his knife, and it let go.

The hobbits dashed inside the gate.

But the Thing in the lake rose up, and with all its might hurled the rock door shut behind them. They would have to go on through the Mines now, in order to get out again.

They began their march through
the Mines. Sam was distraught, for the
pony Bill had fled when the creature
attacked Frodo. 'Poor old Bill,' Sam kept
muttering.

'What was that Thing in the water?'
Aragorn asked Gandalf.

'I do not know. But there are old
and foul creatures in the deep places.'

On and on they journeyed through
the Mines, through caves, across chasms,
up and down great stairways and through
passages elaborately carved and
ornamented. The handiwork of the
dwarves, Gimli's ancestors, was
marvellous to see. Gimli himself hoped to
find dwarves still living in the Mines, most
of all his kinsman Balin, of whom no word
had been heard since he tried to set up a
new kingdom of dwarves here some years
earlier. But no living person was to
be seen.

That night they laid their beds in
an old guard room with a deep well in the
centre. Pippin dropped a stone down it.
'Fool!' said Gandalf. 'Who knows what
you may have woken?' And indeed just

then there began, in the depths, a distant knocking. Pippin listened in horror.

Next day they journeyed on, hoping to reach the gate on the farther side that night. Suddenly they saw daylight. It was streaming down from the roof of a large square chamber into which they had come. In the centre was a great slab of whitened stone.

'A tomb,' said Gandalf, and he read the inscription on it: '*Balin son of Fundin, Lord of Moria.*'

'He is dead, then,' said Gimli. 'I feared it was so.'

'And here is a book,' said Gandalf, picking up tattered and burnt pages, 'which records how he fell. It says that he and his company were attacked by Orcs, foul creatures of Sauron –'

'Hush!' said Legolas. 'I hear drumbeats! Someone is coming!'

Boom, *boom*, rumbled the approaching drums, mingled with cries and the sound of hurrying feet. 'Slam the doors of this chamber!' cried Aragorn, as the Company drew their swords.

They wedged the door against the oncoming attackers, whom they knew now to be Orcs. But even Gandalf's magic could not keep it shut for long. 'There is something else with them,' he panted, 'a great cave-troll, I think.'

A huge arm and shoulder pushed itself through the gap, followed by a great foot. 'The Shire!' cried Frodo, and stabbed at it. But a moment later the door was broken to pieces and Orcs stormed in.

Legolas felled two with arrows and Gimli hewed another with his axe. All fought like demons, but the Company was outnumbered. A huge Orc-chieftain sprang into the room and pinned Frodo to the wall with his spear.

Aragorn slew the Orc, and Frodo was only saved by the mail-shirt which Bilbo had given him, and which he wore next to the skin. 'Run for it!' cried Gandalf.

They fled down the stairs and into a great hall. At the end

of it yawned a fiery chasm, across which stretched a slender bridge. There was no other way out.

Gandalf made them run across the bridge ahead of him, and stood to defend it. The Orcs were swarming in hundreds, and among them rose a terrible shadow. 'Ai!' wailed Legolas. 'A Balrog is come!'

The Balrog reached the bridge and drew itself up to a great height. Only Gandalf stood to bar its way, looking small and alone. The Balrog leapt forward on to the bridge, wielding its whip and its flaming sword. Gandalf lifted his staff and with it cracked the bridge. With a terrible cry the Balrog fell into the abyss, but Gandalf was dragged down with it. 'Fly, you fools!' he cried, and was gone.

The Company gazed in horror. 'Come!' cried Aragorn. 'Follow me, obey him.' They stumbled wildly up the great stairs beyond the bridge and out towards the huge broken gates that led to daylight. Here there crouched a guard of Orcs, but Aragorn smote down their captain, and the rest fled in terror.

So Frodo and his companions came out into the bright sunlight, leaving the shadow of the mountain behind them. Faint drum-beats still sounded in the distance, but they were safe. Yet each of them wept.

Aragorn tended their wounds. 'What does it matter now?' asked Frodo, as he was examined for any hurt. 'We have no hope without Gandalf.'

'Yet we must journey on,' answered Aragorn. 'Why, Frodo, I see now how you escaped death. You are wearing a shirt of dwarvish mithril-silver, which the Orc's spear could not penetrate!'

At last they began to journey on again, travelling towards the forest of Lothlórien, an Elven kingdom of great beauty. 'I can hear something following us now and then,' said Frodo anxiously. 'There have been footsteps behind us ever since we were in Moria.'

'Whatever creature it is,' answered Aragorn, 'it can do us no harm where we are going. Nothing evil passes through Lothlórien.'

'That is not what we say in Gondor,' said Boromir suspiciously. 'We believe this Lothlórien to be perilous.'

'Then you know nothing!' exclaimed Legolas heatedly.

At sunset they came to the trees of Lothlórien, and at last into the presence of its Lady, the Elven-queen Galadriel, and her consort Celeborn.

'My greeting to you all,' said Galadriel, 'and greeting especially to you, Frodo Baggins of the Shire, the Ring-bearer.

Yes, your quest is known to us. Rest here now for a little, until you are healed of your sorrow.'

They remained for days in Lothlórien. All the while that they dwelt there, the sun shone and the air was cool and soft, as if it was early spring. Often they spoke together of Gandalf, and listened while the Elves of Lothlórien sang of the wizard and his deeds, calling him by his elvish name, *Mithrandir,* which means 'Grey Pilgrim'. Yet besides their grief they found happiness there. Boromir and Aragorn practised their skill with swords, and Legolas showed Gimli how to shoot with a bow, while Sam picked marvellous flowers and Merry and Pippin dozed.

At last they knew that they must travel on again. Galadriel led Sam and Frodo to a silver basin of water. 'This is the Mirror of Galadriel,' she told them. 'It shows things that were, and things that are, and things that yet may be. Do you wish to look?'

Sam gazed into it. He saw a strange vision: Frodo lying pale as if dead, himself climbing an endless winding stair, and the trees of his own Shire crashing to the ground. He shivered in horror.

Then it was Frodo's turn, and to him, gazing in the water of the Mirror, there came a vision of an aged man walking down a winding road, clad all in white. 'Gandalf?' whispered Frodo. 'But no, it cannot be.' He saw, too, armies on the march, fire and smoke, the turmoil of battle, and – growing out of these pictures – a single Eye which seemed to search restlessly for him. He felt that he wanted to put on the Ring.

'No!' warned Galadriel. 'You must not. For this is the Eye of Sauron, and he is looking for you. But he cannot find you here.' Then Frodo saw the ring that she wore on her own finger, and knew that it was one of the great Elven-rings made long ago, over which the Dark Lord had no power.

'In the morning you must depart,' said Galadriel. 'Even now the boats which will carry you down the Great River towards Mordor are being made ready for you.'

The Company set out from Lothlórien in three Elf-boats, leaving Galadriel and her kingdom with great sorrow. Even Gimli, who like all dwarves had a deep distrust of elvish peoples, was almost weeping.

They journeyed on by water, and that evening they moored by a small river island, on which they made their evening meal. 'In a few days,' Aragorn told them while they ate, 'we will have to choose. The Dark Lord is waging war against Gondor in the west, and Boromir wishes to return to the aid of his people. Shall we go with him, or shall we turn east to Mordor and its Shadow? Or should we break our fellowship and go this way and that as each desires? We must choose very soon.'

The days passed, and they journeyed on down the river. On each side, the cliffs rose steadily higher, until there came in view two great pillars of stone, shaped into the likeness of mighty kings. 'These are the Argonath,' said Aragorn, 'the Pillars of the Kings. They are Isildur and Anarion, my fathers of old.'

The next day the Company drew their boats up on the bank, and Aragorn told them: 'The hour has come at last when we must choose. What is to become of our fellowship?'

Frodo begged for an hour alone, to make his decision. He walked away from the others, out of sight into the trees.

For a long while he sat by himself, in confusion and no nearer to a decision. Suddenly he felt that he was being watched, and, springing to his feet, saw that Boromir had followed him. 'Frodo,' said Boromir, 'you must come to Gondor with me, so that we may use the Ring to defend my land against the enemy from Mordor.'

'I cannot,' said Frodo, 'for whatever is done with the Ring turns to evil.'

'Then,' cried Boromir, his face suddenly contorted with rage and madness, 'give *me* the Ring!' And he leapt at Frodo.

Springing back from Boromir, Frodo put on the Ring, and vanished from sight.

Boromir gasped in amazement. Then he began to run wildly about, searching for Frodo, until he tripped and fell sprawling. Weeping now, he cried: 'Frodo, come back! A madness took me, but it has passed.'

There came no answer. Boromir got slowly to his feet and returned to the others. 'Have you seen Frodo?' Aragorn asked him.

'I tried to convince him to come to Gondor,' answered Boromir slowly. 'I grew angry, and he vanished. He must have put on the Ring.'

'This is bad!' cried Sam, jumping up. 'Mr Frodo! Where are you?' And he dashed off. The others followed him, and soon overtook him. Suddenly a thought crossed his mind. 'The boats,' he muttered. 'That's where he'll be.' And he ran back to the river bank.

Sure enough, a boat was moving off all by itself. 'Coming, Mr Frodo!' called Sam. 'Wait for me!' He tossed his pack into the boat, and jumped. But he missed the boat by a yard, and the water closed over his head. Struggling in utter panic, he spluttered: 'Save me, Mr Frodo! I'm drownded!'

An invisible hand reached down for him and pulled him into the boat. Then Frodo took off the Ring. 'Well, Sam,' he said, laughing, 'you are a confounded nuisance. Don't hinder me, for I am going to Mordor.'

'Of course, Mr Frodo,' answered Sam. 'And I'm coming with you.' Their boat drew away from the shore.

Not far behind them in the water, unobserved by them, swam something that was following them. It was black, like a log, and had pale luminous eyes, the eyes that Bilbo had once seen in the cave of Gollum.

'Frodo! Frodo!' called Merry and Pippin, still searching among the trees for their cousin. Suddenly without warning they were surrounded by Orcs.

    They put up a struggle, and managed to wound several who had ambushed them, but they were hopelessly unequal. Yet it seemed that the foul creatures wanted to capture them unharmed rather than to wound or kill.

Suddenly a big sword slashed into the throng of Orcs. Boromir had arrived. Placing his body between the hobbits and their attackers, he drove the Orcs back, fighting like a man possessed. He killed six or seven Orcs, and the rest turned and fled.

Clutching Merry and Pippin, Boromir began to lead them to safety, when a sudden rain of Orc-arrows fell, piercing him in many places. Even so, he fought on, roaring with fury and slashing out at this new wave of attackers.

At last he began to grow weak, though he had slain many Orcs. With his last strength, he lifted his great horn and blew a mighty blast on it.

Far away, Aragorn, who was still hunting for Frodo, heard it and cried 'Boromir!' Racing down the slopes – where Legolas and Gimli too were struggling against a swarm of Orcs – he reached the clearing and saw Boromir lying wounded. There was no sign of Merry or Pippin.

'I – I tried to take the Ring,' panted Boromir. 'I have paid for it. Aragorn go to Gondor, save my people.'

'I will,' answered Aragorn. 'But what of the hobbits?'

'Of Frodo and Sam I know nothing. The others – Orcs took them – I think they are alive.' And Boromir fell silent.

'He is dead,' said Aragorn.

Aragorn, Legolas and Gimli laid Boromir in a boat and set it adrift. 'Let the River take him,' said Aragorn. 'And now we must search for Merry and Pippin.'

'Should we not follow Frodo?' asked Legolas. 'I see from the footprints that he and Sam have taken a boat. They must be heading for Mordor.'

'Their fate is in their hands,' said Aragorn. 'We must hope to rescue the others.' And he, Legolas and Gimli ran off through the woods, following the trampled and littered trail of the Orcs.

They ran on for many hours, but the Orcs were moving swiftly too, and there were many miles between pursuers and pursued. Aragorn and Gimli grew deathly tired, and though Legolas had no weariness as he ran, he was full of doubt and dread as to what they might find.

As to Merry and Pippin, they were in a bad way. Merry, who had been injured in the fight, was being carried by an Orc, but Pippin was being forced to run, driven on with a whip, until at last he collapsed.

'Filth! Maggots!' jeered one of the Orc leaders. 'Can't run!' He fingered his long jagged blade.

Just then there was an alarm. A band of horsemen from the land of Rohan, on whose borders they now were, had sighted the Orcs and was attacking them. All was confusion. At this moment one of the Orcs decided to sneak off with Merry and Pippin by himself, in hopes of getting the Ring, which he believed they were carrying. Then this Orc was felled by an arrow shot by a horseman of Rohan. Snatching his sword, Merry and Pippin cut themselves free from their bonds, just managing to escape being trampled by the horses. 'Well,' panted Merry as they ran off, 'we're free!'

'This is Fangorn Forest,' panted Merry, pointing at the huge trees which overshadowed them.

'Fangorn?' said Pippin, alarmed. 'That's supposed to be a very sinister place. We're no safer here than with the Orcs.'

'Well, we shall see,' said Merry. 'Come on!' And together they fled into the forest.

The great trees loomed over them. They scrambled up a hill, and settled down to rest on the roots of an old tree stump that had only two branches left. 'It

doesn't seem so terrible here after all,' admitted Pippin. 'In fact I almost feel I like the place.'

'Almost feel you like the Forest?' boomed a deep voice directly above them. 'That's uncommonly kind of you.'

Merry and Pippin froze with terror. When at last they dared to look up, they found they were staring into the face of a huge figure, partly man-like or troll-like, but chiefly tree. They had been sitting in its hands. 'What are you?' gasped Pippin.

'*Hoom, Hoom,*' answered the huge creature in a voice like a deep woodwind instrument. 'You speak hastily. I am an Ent, or that is what they call me. Fangorn is my name according to some, and Treebeard others make it. Treebeard will do. But you are in my country, and I should be doing the asking. What are you, I wonder?'

'We are hobbits,' answered Merry, 'and our names are Merry and Pippin, and we got caught by Orcs, and they dragged us all the way here, and we escaped from them, and ran into your forest, and —'

'You *are* hasty folk,' said Treebeard. 'You must tell me your story at the proper speed. Orcs, you say? *Hrum,* I am no friend of those tree-killing beasts and their masters. You must tell me more. We will go to my home.' And he lifted them up in his great hands, and began to stride through the forest with them.

Meanwhile Aragorn, Legolas and Gimli had reached the outskirts of Fangorn Forest and had found signs of the battle between the Riders of Rohan and the Orcs. They spotted the tracks of Merry and Pippin, and traced them into the forest.

'They disappear suddenly here,' said Legolas, puzzled. 'It is as if they had been snatched into the air.'

'Look!' cried Gimli in sudden alarm. An old man was approaching them up the hill, leaning on a staff. 'It is Saruman, I am certain. Shoot, before he puts a spell on us!'

Legolas raised his bow and bent it. The old man spoke without looking up. 'Elf, Man and Dwarf together? A rare sight in these troubled times. Well met, my friends.'

'Saruman,' threatened Gimli, raising his axe, 'what have you done with Merry and Pippin?'

Suddenly the old man sprang upon a rock. His grey rags slipped away to reveal garments of shining white. The three companions cried aloud with joy. 'Gandalf!' shouted Aragorn unbelievingly. 'Beyond all hope, Gandalf!' The old man frowned, as though remembering with difficulty.

'Yes, Gandalf was my name.'

'What happened to you?' asked Legolas. 'Did you slay the Balrog?'

'Name him not!' said Gandalf with terrible intensity. 'Long time we fell, and his fire was about me. I was burned. Ever he clutched me, and ever I hewed him, far under the living earth, until at last he fled back up the secret ways of Moria. There we fought, above the mists of the world, and the mountain was wreathed

with lightning. At last I threw down my enemy, and his fall broke the mountainside. Then darkness took me, and I wandered far on roads that I will not tell . . . And now I have been sent back for a brief time, until my task is done. It is time that I was about it! Come, we must ride to Théoden, king of Rohan.'

'I rode with King Théoden when I was young,' said Aragorn as he and his companions rode towards Edoras, the chief city of Rohan. 'He was a mighty prince.'

'Théoden is old now,' said Gandalf, 'and he leaves everything in the hands of his minister, Wormtongue. And thanks to this Wormtongue, Rohan is not mustering its forces as it should, to meet the attack from Saruman at Isengard, which I know is coming. Something must be done!'

At the castle of Théoden it was as Gandalf had foretold. Wormtongue watched over his master Théoden. Near the throne there stood also a young woman of the royal blood, proud and lovely. Her name was Eowyn, and she looked long at Aragorn.

Gandalf greeted the old king in the tongue of Rohan. '*Westu Théoden hál!* It is time for us to gather together against the power of Mordor and its puppet Saruman. Hear me!'

It was Wormtongue who answered. 'It is I who counsel the king now, Gandalf Stormcrow,' he said sneeringly, 'and he hears you no longer.'

—'Be quiet, Grima Wormtongue!' cried Gandalf in a terrible voice. 'How long is it since Saruman bought you? Down, snake! Down on your belly!'

Wormtongue drew a knife and was about to leap at Gandalf, but the wizard raised his staff, and there was a flash like lightning from its tip. Wormtongue was thrown on his face, where he lay, alive but helpless.

'And now,' said Gandalf, turning to Théoden, 'take courage, Lord of Rohan. Do not wait for Saruman's attack. Send your Riders to halt the forces of Isengard at the old fortress of Helm's Deep.'

Théoden stood up tall and straight, looking almost young again. 'So be it!' he cried.

'And I will lead them. Bring me my armour!'

n the third day after they had left the others, Frodo and Sam were scrambling down a deep ravine. 'Thank goodness for that rope the Elves gave you, Sam,' said Frodo. 'We'd never have got down without it.'

Sam peered into the distance. 'There's that Mount Doom flickering again in Mordor,' he said. 'The one place in the world that we don't want to be, and that's where we're trying to go. And if you ask me at the present moment we're well and truly lost.'

'Hush,' said Frodo suddenly.

Above them, on the edge of the ravine, they could hear a hissing voice: 'Sss! Cautious, my preciousss!' Two pale green eyes peered down at the hobbits.

'Yes, it's him,' whispered Frodo. 'It's Gollum, who once had the Ring. He has been following us since Moria, I think.'

'Well,' said Sam grimly, 'he'll be sorry he found us.' He and Frodo crept into the shadow of the cliff.

Slowly, foothold by foothold, down came Gollum, clinging to the cliff with his hands and toes, snuffling and mumbling to himself. 'Where iss it, my preciousss? It's ours, and we wants it.'

Suddenly Sam was upon him. 'Got you!' he cried. But Gollum was more than he bargained for. With a horrible rubbery strength, he pinned Sam's arms and legs and began feeling for his throat. Frodo came to the rescue, jerking the creature's head back and holding his sword at its throat.

'Let go, Gollum,' he said, 'or I'll cut your throat.'

Whimpering and grovelling, Gollum collapsed utterly. 'Don't hurt us, don't let them hurt us, preciousss! We'll be nice to them, *Gollum*, very nice to them if they'll be nice to us. Hobbits won't kill us, will they? Nice hobbits!'

'No, we won't kill you,' said Frodo. 'But we won't let you go either. You will have to come with us and be our guide. You must lead us to Mordor.'

'Ach!' cried Gollum. 'Sss! No, precious, not to Mordor. Hobbits mustn't go there!' And he made a frog-like bound into the darkness. But Frodo and Sam pounced, and recaptured him. At first they tied him up with the elven-rope, but Gollum cried out that it hurt him, and Frodo believed this.

'Sméagol will be very good,' said Gollum in a different tone of voice, using his old name. 'Sméagol promises never to let *Him* have the Preciousss. Sméagol will serve you, good master!' And he began to weep and bite at the rope.

The hobbits took it off, and now Gollum began to frisk about Frodo, like a dog inviting his master for a walk. 'Off we go,' he whimpered. 'Follow Sméagol! Sméagol knows a secret way, he does, across the Marshes. Follow Sméagol!'

Gollum moved quickly, with his head and neck thrust forward, often using his hands as well as his feet. Frodo and Sam were hard put to it to keep up with him, but he seemed no longer to have any thought of escaping, and if they fell behind, he would turn and wait for them.

They came to the foul Marshes that lay across their path, and began to thread their way through a network of pools and soft mires, from which their rose a rotting vapour. Through it, now and then, they could glimpse the ominous shapes of the mountains of Mordor.

Once, there was a terrible moment when a black shadow came out of Mordor towards them in the sky, giving a high chilling wail as it passed. 'A wraith!' whispered Gollum. 'Wraith on wings! The Preciousss is calling to it!' But the winged Ringwraith went its way and passed out of sight.

Frodo and Sam slept when they could. And as they did so, Gollum would watch them with his luminous eyes. 'Sméagol promised never to let Him have the Preciousss,' he whispered. 'But we wants it! We wants it! And we thinks we knows how to get it . . .'

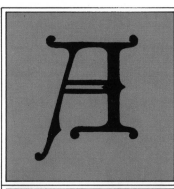

ll this time at Isengard, the forces of Saruman were preparing for battle. Companies of Saruman's own Orcs, with his emblem, the White Hand, on their armour, were forming up in ranks. The whole citadel bustled with wicked energy and anger.

On the steps of the black, impregnable tower of Orthanc stood Saruman himself, directing the preparations. Wormtongue, once the counsellor of Théoden, stood by his side, for Théoden had shown mercy and allowed him to go free. Wormtongue had now crept back to his true master.

'Our time is at hand!' cried Saruman.

The walls of Isengard answered him with savage shouting.

'Théoden's mere hundreds', he cried, 'will face our tens of thousands.'

There was another great cheer.

'And when all the land of Rohan, our ancient oppressor, lies vanquished, then shall we fly further afield, and sweep all of Middle-earth beneath our feet!'

Again, a huge shout answered him.

'We cannot be defeated!' cried Saruman. 'In a mere two days, Théoden's fortress of Edoras will be ours!'

There was a final deafening shout. Horns blew, and the great gates of Isengard were thrown open. Out to battle marched the ranks of the White Hand.

rom the gates of Edoras, Théoden led his men out to battle, riding at the head of his army. The crowd cheered him with joy in their hearts.

Aragorn, Gandalf, Legolas and Gimli rode near him, Gimli on the horse of Legolas. There also rode with them the Lady Eowyn, clad in white mail. But Gandalf soon left them. 'Look for me at Helm's Deep!' he called to Théoden, and rode away on his great stallion Shadowfax.

'Aragorn?' called Théoden to his companion.

'My lord?'

'Is there any hope for us?'

'A small hope, Théoden king,' answered Aragorn, 'a small and lonely hope. The Shadow is already growing over Mordor.' And indeed a darkness seemed to be creeping out of Mordor into the sky.

It was many leagues' ride to the ancient fortress of Helm's Deep. Night fell, and they still rode on.

They were in a low valley when cries and hornblasts were heard from their scouts that went in front. Word came that the hosts of Isengard were already hurrying towards them.

They reached Helm's Deep, and mustered their forces on the Deeping Wall which defended the fortress. 'I like this place,' muttered Gimli. 'And my axe is restless in my hand. Give me a row of orc-necks and room to swing, and all weariness will fall from me.'

Suddenly a flash of lighning lit up the approaches to Helm's Deep. The vast armies of Isengard could be seen all around. 'They come!' cried the men of Rohan.

All that night, the battle raged at Helm's Deep. The forces of Rohan fought bitterly and without wearying, but they were outnumbered by Orcs and were weakened by the machines and terrible devices of Saruman.

As the dawn came, Théoden, exhausted as he was, and knowing that he faced defeat, determined to make a final desperate charge with Aragorn at his side. Out rushed his small band of horsemen – and at that moment a strange sight met their eyes. Where there had been rolling countryside now stood a forest of vast and ancient trees (the people of Treebeard, though Théoden did not know it). And there too was Gandalf, leading a band of Riders whom he had summoned from a far distance. And so the forces of Isengard were defeated.

Gollum had at last brought Frodo and Sam to a secret way into Mordor.

'This is safe, a secret place,' he hissed at them. 'Sméagol's secret way through the black mountains into *His* land. The Straight Stair first, and then the Winding Stair. Follow good Sméagol!'

'And what comes after the Straight Stair and the Winding Stair, Gollum?' asked Sam suspiciously.

'We shall see, Precious,' said Gollum softly. 'Oh yes, we shall see.'

*Here ends the first part
of the
History of the War of the Ring*